GOD, EVIL,
AND
SUFFERING

COMPACT EXPOSITORY PULPIT COMMENTARY SERIES

GOD, EVIL, AND SUFFERING

Understanding God's Role in Tragedies and Atrocities

DAVID A. HARRELL

© 2019 David A. Harrell

ISBN 978-0-9600203-6-2

Great Writing Publications, 425 Roberts Road, Taylors, SC 29687 www.greatwriting.org

Shepherd's Fire 5245 Highway 41-A Joelton, TN 37080 www.shepherdsfire.com

All Scripture quotations, unless stated otherwise, are taken from the New American Standard Bible® (NASB), Copyright © 1960, 1962, 1963, 1968, 1971, 1972, 1973, 1975, 1977, 1995 by The Lockman Foundation. Used by permission. www.Lockman. org All rights reserved.

No part of this publication may be reproduced, or stored in a retrieval system, or transmitted, in any form or by any means, mechanical, electronic, photocopying, recording or otherwise, without the prior permission of the publishers.

Shepherd's Fire exists to proclaim the unsearchable riches of Christ through mass communications for the teaching ministry of Bible expositor David Harrell, with a special emphasis in encouraging and strengthening pastors and church leaders.

Contents

	Introduction..7
1	Compatabilistic Theodicy................................23
2	Three Competing Theological Systems..........27
3	The Reformed Position..32
4	God's Glory and the Origin of Sin..................38
5	The Tragedy and Atrocity of the Crucifixion....48
6	God's Role in Israel's Unbelief.........................52
7	Three Reasons God Ordained to Allow Evil..57
8	All Things for Good..67
9	What God May Be Up to in Our Suffering.....72
10	Final Words of Encouragement.......................80

Books in this Series

Finding Grace in Sorrow: Enduring Trials with the Joy of the Holy Spirit

Finding Strength in Weakness: Drawing Upon the Existing Grace Within

Glorifying God in Your Body: Seeing Ourselves from God's Perspective

God, Evil, and Suffering: Understanding God's Role in Tragedies and Atrocities

God's Gracious Gift of Assurance: Rediscovering the Benefits of Justification by Faith

Our Sin and the Savior: Understanding the Need for Renewing and Sanctifying Grace

The Marvel of Being in Christ: Adoring God's Loving Provision of New Life in the Spirit

The Miracle of Spiritual Sight: Affirming the Transforming Doctrine of Regeneration

Introduction

As every Christian can affirm, Bible study groups can be frustrating. Whether in a traditional Sunday school setting or a friend's living room, studying Scripture can easily digress from a warm exchange of theological pleasantries into a spirited debate, then digress into heated disagreements. I remember such an occasion in a large Sunday school class I visited soon after I had graduated from seminary.

The teacher was a kind and gentle man, long on love but short on theological acumen. His method of teaching was typical of many well-meaning lay teachers. He was basically a group facilitator who relied heavily on the Sunday School curriculum notes supplied by his denomination that were carefully crafted to avoid anything that might be considered controversial. With no emphasis on exegetical or contextual considerations or any appeal to sound doctrine, the content was as shallow as water on a plate, a mixture of psychology, sociology, philosophy, and anecdotes. The lesson writers had an uncanny ability to make the obvious even more obvious, causing the student to be comfortable, even smug, in his or her perceived theological prowess. It was yet another example of how to market the faith as if it were some cheap commodity for those who want a personalized spirituality rather than an accurate theology anchored in sound doctrine that would produce a genuine devotion to the glory of God and an ever-deepening love of the Lord whose "lovingkindness is better than life" (Ps. 63:3).

As the class enjoyed their coffee and doughnuts and bantered about various ideas, it was obvious no one had a firm grasp of Scripture. With the theological depth and accuracy of the average Facebook post, it was basically an opportunity for the people there to voice their opinions—each considered to be equally valid, no matter how strange, contradictory, or unbiblical. Not once did anyone refer to a passage of Scripture as the basis for his or her position. In fact, to my dismay, most of the class did not even have a Bible. They only had their lesson manual.

Eventually, to the consternation of the teacher, the ebb and flow of a very boring conversation drifted into the issue of God's role in evil and suffering, and the origin of sin. Suddenly, like dowsing a bunch of sleepyheads with cold water, the whole class came alive. But I truly felt sorry for the teacher. He unexpectedly found himself in a very uncomfortable position when one lady asked a question that went something like this: "If God is a loving God, if He is sovereign over everything, and if He hates sin, why is there so much evil and suffering in the world?"

It was obvious from the tone of her voice and the redness in her face that she was looking for a fight. She had more than a theological bee in her bonnet. Her question was clearly an expression of pent-up anger. I didn't know it at the time, but I later learned why. She and her husband had recently lost a child to terminal illness after several years of suffering, surgeries, and immeasurable heartache.

After a pregnant silence in the room, she added, "I just don't understand why a loving God would allow our innocent little boy to suffer for years, and then die." As if rehearsed, the rest of the class immediately nodded their heads and warmly grunted their shared concern with an uneasy sense of, "Gotcha!" Her question obviously struck a nerve. Although they did not express it, they were all starving for a way to make sense out of how a loving God who is supposedly in control of all things and knows all things can allow the daily tragedies and atrocities we all witness and even experience.

Instantly the insipid conversation disappeared, and the class was electrified with curiosity.

Caught off-guard and clueless, the teacher played the card many teachers have up their sleeve and answered professorially, "That's a great question!" Clearly at a loss for words he then added, "That's not part of our lesson today, but let's talk about that for a minute. How would you answer that? Anyone?" What happened next was nothing short of the pooling of ignorance. It was armchair theology at its very worst. It reminded me of the old adage, "Opinions are like noses: everyone's got one."

Sadly, all their opinions were offered as if they were seated in a courtroom and God was on trial for being unjust, impotent, both, or even outright indifferent. Worse yet, their arguments were based upon the assumption that man's happiness (rooted in his depraved human desires) is the center of gravity around which God must orbit. Fallen human wisdom, rather than God's revelation in Scripture, was their standard for divine justice and mercy. The idea that God is all-powerful and all-good, has the right to do whatever He pleases, has no need to defend His actions, places the blame of evil in the world on Satan and sinners, and calls sinful man to repentant faith in Christ as the only remedy for evil were concepts utterly foreign to the conversation.

While none of them (including the lay teacher) had a biblical understanding of the issue, I did appreciate their desire to grapple with it. I remember thinking and praying earnestly that they would eventually understand that the solution to the existence of evil and suffering in the world must be *theocentric*, not *anthropocentric*, which is at the very heart of Paul's comforting statement: "And we know that God causes all things to work together for good to those who love God, to those who are called according to *His* purpose" (Rom. 8:28)—a passage I'm sure they all knew from memory, but obviously had no grasp of its ultimate meaning.

I found myself in an awkward position. I wanted to defend what I was convinced to be the truth found in Scripture. But being a visitor, I thought it might be presumptuous. So I bit my tongue—at least for a while. Finally, I could stand it no longer. So I held up my hand and asked if I could humbly offer another position for their consideration. Of course, the teacher kindly agreed. Knowing only a few of them had a Bible, I read to them Paul's words in Romans 9:23-24 and briefly explained what I will elaborate upon later in this book.

After admitting that I certainly did not claim to have all the answers, that indeed "the secret things belong to the Lord" (Deut. 29:29) and "[His] thoughts are not [our] thoughts, nor are [His] ways [our] ways" (Isa. 55:8), I recall asking the class a series of questions that went something like this:

- Do you think it is possible that God actually ordained to allow evil to enter His perfect creation to put His glory on display in ways that could have never happened apart from the existence of evil?
- Is it possible that God ultimately uses evil for good? Isn't that what Romans 8:28 tells us?
- Is it possible that God is more concerned about His eternal glory than man's temporal happiness?
- Is it possible that God is more glorified with evil existing in the world, than if that were not the case? We know, for example, that according to Acts 4:27, God predetermined the murder of His beloved Son.

While my questions and very brief instruction were met with tepid enthusiasm, it did strike a chord with some, especially the teacher. As a result, he asked me to address the class at a future date to explain these matters more fully. In the providence of God, that happened several weeks later. In fact, the size of the class doubled (as word got around) and it led to several other subsequent mini-lectures on the subject. I wish I could say that eventually everyone agreed and we all lived happily ever after, but that was not the case. However, through the sanctifying work of the Holy Spirit and His Word, some were forever changed and remain thankful to this day for what they learned from Scripture. For indeed, "All Scripture is inspired by God and profitable for teaching, for reproof, for correction, for training in righteousness; that the man of God may be adequate; equipped for every good work" (2 Tim. 3:16-17). For those I saw shaking their heads in disagreement, I suppose all I did was spit in their theological soup. While they may continue to enjoy their delicious concoction, I'm sure it never tasted as good as it once did.

God's Right to be Trusted

Frankly, the very concept of evil is seldom considered, especially in our postmodern culture that rejects moral absolutes and has no understanding of right and wrong from God's perspective. Therefore, to somehow *trust* God, even in the face of gratuitous evil is considered by most to be quite absurd. It was fascinating, however, to see how often the word "evil" was suddenly the dominant term used to describe the Islamic jihadist's terrorist attacks on US soil on September 11, 2001. Unfortunately, but not unexpectedly, since evil had no moral category in which to exist—and since it was politically incorrect to consider any people group to be "evil"—the term itself was gradually discarded. But what was really intriguing was the effect that that act of evil had upon the American perspective of the *goodness of God*. David Wells illustrates this well:

> ... one of the casualties of September 11 appears to have been God himself. Before the terrorist attacks, 72% of Americans affirmed their belief that God is omnipotent and in control of the world, but afterwards that figure dropped to 68%. And just before the attacks occurred, 38% affirmed their belief in moral absolutes which are true for all times and places and not determined by circumstance, but in the days immediately following the attack only 22% were willing to affirm that. The language of evil had become a verbal necessity after September 11, but it remained a cultural and conceptual difficulty. That this was the case was all too evident a year later when signs were popping up all over the cultural landscape suggesting that outrage over the attack was out of order. . . . Without moral absolutes, the business of making moral judgments becomes impossible, although few seemed to see the anomaly that was at work: that those who take

the position that judgments should not be rendered on behavior are, often unbeknownst to themselves, also taking a moral position.[1]

Trusting God, come what may, is at the very heart of the Christian faith. But it goes against our nature, especially when we experience evil, whether it's physical or moral.

The account of Job portrays this struggle, even in a man who was considered to be the most righteous on earth—a man compared with Noah and Daniel (Ezek. 14:14-20); a man of whom God said, "For there is no one like him on the earth, a blameless and upright man, fearing God and turning away from evil" (Job 1:8).

In that fascinating historical account revealed to us by the Spirit of God through His inspired author (perhaps Moses or Solomon), Satan refutes God's claims of Job's righteousness, insisting Job's faith and obedience were merely a manipulative ploy to gain divine blessings. But God knew otherwise. He knew that Job's righteousness was not that of his own, but a supernatural gift of God given to bring glory to Himself. Knowing how he had seduced the holy angels to join his original rebellion (cf. Isa. 14:12ff.; Ezek. 28:11ff.; Rev. 12:4), Satan probably assumed he would have no problem doing the same with Job—or any other person who trusted God. No doubt he believed that if he could inflict enough suffering and pain, Job would "curse God and die!" (Job 2:9)—as his wife later counseled him to do.

So with the purpose of proving Satan wrong and thereby proving the unfailing power of genuine saving faith, He consented to allow Satan to test Job. While Job's faith never failed (see 13:15), it did falter under the weight of unexplained, undeserved, and unbearable suffering and loss. As the pain and sorrow increased, Job repeatedly called God to court in order to verify his innocence. We see this, for example, in the following passages:

> I loathe my own life;
> I will give full vent to my complaint;
> I will speak in the bitterness of my soul.
> "I will say to God, 'Do not condemn me;
> Let me know why You contend with me.
> 'Is it right for You indeed to oppress,
> To reject the labor of Your hands,
> And to look favorably on the schemes of the wicked?
> 'Have You eyes of flesh?
> Or do You see as a man sees?
> Are Your days as the days of a mortal,
> Or Your years as man's years,
> That You should seek for my guilt
> And search after my sin?

According to Your knowledge I am indeed not guilty,
Yet there is no deliverance from Your hand
(Job 10:1-7).

Even today my complaint is rebellion;
His hand is heavy despite my groaning.
Oh that I knew where I might find Him,
That I might come to His seat!
I would present *my* case before Him
And fill my mouth with arguments.
I would learn the words *which* He would answer,
And perceive what He would say to me.
Would He contend with me by the greatness of *His* power?
No, surely He would pay attention to me.
There the upright would reason with Him;
And I would be delivered forever from my Judge
(Job 23:1-7).

But what is truly fascinating is that never once did God give Job an audience to present his case. Never once did God even explain how He had squared off with Satan to prove how saving faith cannot be destroyed, no matter how severe the tragedies and atrocities, and how he (Job) was the test case to forever substantiate His divine assertion. Never once did God allow Himself to be dragged into court by

His sinful creatures. Instead, He responded to Job's demand for a judicial hearing by intimidating him with His glory! He began by saying,

> Then the LORD answered Job out of the whirlwind and said,
> "Who is this that darkens counsel
> By words without knowledge?
> "Now gird up your loins like a man,
> And I will ask you, and you instruct Me!
> "Where were you when I laid the foundation of the earth?
> Tell *Me,* if you have understanding,
> Who set its measurements? Since you know.
> Or who stretched the line on it?
> "On what were its bases sunk?
> Or who laid its cornerstone,
> When the morning stars sang together
> And all the sons of God shouted for joy?"
> (Job 38:1-7).

The sheer force of God's intimidation and humiliation put Job in his place (as it does all of us). Job was forced to face the reality that no matter how severe and inexplicably unfair the trial, *God is never to be challenged. He is only to be trusted*. For He alone is the Creator, Sustainer, Controller, Redeemer, and Consummator of all things. Job learned that to even question such a transcendent, omniscient, omnipotent God was the height of folly, and he became deeply convicted that to be so presumptuous as to even insinuate that God is unfair was an act of high treason against the Most High.

Then, as expected, Job humbled himself before God, even though he had lost everything except his life, and he said this:

> I know that You can do all things,
> And that no purpose of Yours can be thwarted.
> "Who is this that hides counsel without knowledge?"
> Therefore I have declared that which I did not understand,
> Things too wonderful for me, which I did not know.
> "Hear, now, and I will speak;
> I will ask You, and You instruct me."
> I have heard of You by the hearing of the ear;
> But now my eye sees You;
> Therefore I retract,
> And I repent in dust and ashes
> (Job 42:2-6).

Though his circumstances had not changed, his perspective had changed drastically. His presumptuous pride and ignorance gave way to humility and wisdom. All the answers he and his friends concocted to explain God's reasons for inflicting so much suffering on him were worthless and mistaken, worthy only of God's rebuke (42:7). In fact, God never gave him an explanation—not only because He didn't owe him one, but also because Job couldn't understand it if He did. Why the innocent suffer is an inscrutable mystery known only to God who has ordained it for purposes that ultimately inure to His glory—a lesson we all must learn. The tragic consequences of living in a fallen, sin-cursed world are inevitable, albeit more severe for some than others—a reality that should cause every believer to hate sin all the more and rejoice in the certain hope that we will one day be delivered from every appearance and effect of evil.

Then, as if to demonstrate His unfailing love and compassion, God restored Job's health, fortunes, and family; when he prayed for his friends, "the LORD increased all that he had twofold" (42:10). James' commentary on Job's ordeal underscores God's compassion and mercy when he says, "We count those blessed who endured. You have heard of the endurance of Job and have seen the outcome of the Lord's dealings, that the Lord is full of compassion and *is* merciful" (James 5:11).

From this amazing real-life illustration that God

has graciously given to us, we can see most vividly that *God has a right to be trusted, and He is worthy to be trusted*. And can there be any greater comfort than knowing we will one day bask in the fullness of His goodness for eternity? I think not. The perfections of His attributes and the magnitude of His sovereign power are exceedingly beyond anything we can possibly comprehend. His ineffable glory and eternal grace humble us to the core. We must therefore bow our heads in breathless adoration and acknowledge that we as creatures have no right to question our Creator. He has the right to do as He pleases. Because of this, when we find ourselves in some crucible of grace, we must never ask, "Why?" We must only ask, "What?" "What can I do to demonstrate my unfailing trust in You, my God?" Then with Moses relax and say, "The secret things belong to the Lord" (Deut. 29:29). We must say, "I cannot possibly understand Your plans and purposes, nor could I comprehend them if You were to explain them. So I will curse sin and praise You for every expression of Your goodness even in my sorrow and pain, casting all my anxiety on You, because You care for me" (1 Peter 5:7).

By considering the manifestation of these great truths in the life of Job, and many other characters in Scripture, we are humbled by the following truths that should permeate our heart, especially in days of trouble:

- There are matters going on in heaven with God that believers know nothing about; yet, they affect their lives;
- Even the best effort at explaining the issues of life can be useless;
- God's people do suffer. Bad things happen all the time to good people, so one cannot judge a person's spirituality by his painful circumstances or successes;
- Even though God seems far away, perseverance in faith is a most noble virtue since God is good and one can safely leave one's life in His hands;
- The believer in the midst of suffering should not abandon God, but draw near to Him, so out of the fellowship can come the comfort — without the explanation;
- Suffering may be intense, but it will ultimately end for the righteous and God will bless abundantly.[2]

1

Compatibilistic Theodicy

Technically, this subject falls under the efforts of *theodicy*: the vindication of divine goodness and providence in view of the existence of evil. The term *theodicy* comes from the Greek *theos* ("god"), and *dikē* ("justice"). Combined, they express a "judicial hearing of God" or the "justification of God."

Like the frustrated folks in the Sunday school class, people attempt to either *attack* or *rescue* the character of God for allowing evil to enter His perfect creation for reasons He never fully discloses. In fact, God makes no attempt to justify His actions; nor is He subject to any human court, though man tends to put Him on trial by using principles of justice based upon his own fallen wisdom and desires rather than the principles God has revealed in His Word that accurately describe His person and works. But when considering God's role in evil and suffering, *we must accept the compatibilism of the infinite love and goodness of God even in the presence of evil* (as we do the same when considering God's sovereignty and man's responsibility).

In light of this, it is noteworthy that nowhere in Scripture does God provide any clear explanation of the origin of evil and His purposes in it, yet He affirms His goodness and love on virtually every page of holy writ. The absence of such a defense speaks to His unwillingness to stand before the biased bar of fallen human reason and justice. It also serves as a rebuke to all who would dare shake their fists in God's face and demand that He defend Himself. Robert Culver is helpful in this regard:

> There is no passage of Scripture which speaks directly and clearly to the subject of the origin of evil and of Satan. It is a matter of considerable importance that the Bible nowhere attempts to justify God (theodicy) in allowing evil in the created world. The book of Job is sometimes supposed to explain its presence and to justify God. The denouement (chap. 38-42) show God cannot be summoned like a defendant and forced to bear witness against Himself. No extreme of suffering gives mere man license to question God's wisdom or justice as Job had done. It is apparently on this very point that Job repents and recants. Yet, however

> much Job may tell the devout believer about right reactions to those "natural" evils (loss of property, family, health and the like), which a pagan cosmology calls "misfortune" or "bad luck," the book never once attempts either to blame God or to justify Him in letting it all happen. Rather God, who all the time is known (by the reader, who is let in on the conspiracy, so to speak) to be benevolent, omnipotent and omniscient, is acknowledged by a believing, but most fractious patriarch, to be so. The focus of interest is not the presence of evil in the world, but a good man's response to evil.[3]

For this reason, we must humbly acknowledge that our best efforts to vindicate His goodness and providence in view of the existence of evil will be woefully inadequate. However, Scripture does give us some general categories that give us a basic understanding—doctrinal truths that should be examined with a spiritual gravitas worthy of such a sublime topic. For here we try to understand the transcendent perfections of our infinitely Holy God who, as in the case of Moses on Mount Sinai, has only allowed us to see the veiled back side of His glory.

My attempt here will be to deal with this very simply and avoid the complicated and often tortured arguments of the philosophical disciplines of ethics, axiology (values), and the theological disciplines of philosophy of religion and apologetics.[4] While volumes have been written on this subject, my purpose is to provide a concise overview of the subject that will hopefully provide the necessary theological foundation for those who wish to study further, but also offer sufficient instruction to bring clarity and comfort to those in need. What we will see, as D. A. Carson states, is that

> God is less interested in answering our questions than in other things: securing our allegiance, establishing our faith, nurturing a desire for holiness. An important part of spiritual maturity is bound up with this obvious truth. God tells us a great deal about himself; but the mysteries that remain are not going to be answered at a merely theoretical and intellectual level. We may probe a little around the edges, using the minds God has given us to glimpse something of his glory. But ultimately the Christian will take refuge from questions about God not in proud, omniscient explanations but in adoring worship.[5]

2

Three Competing Theological Systems

In retrospect, I realized that the various positions of the Sunday School class represented three common theological systems found among evangelicals—two very popular and one commonly despised and misrepresented. Although they did not realize it, some aligned themselves with the tenets of *Process Theology*, a contemporary philosophical system that denies the sovereignty and immutability of God (among other orthodox Christian doctrines), believing instead that God is forever changing and learning in response to the cosmic processes of the universe, and that He reacts accordingly. They would argue that God was surprised when Satan rebelled against Him, and equally shocked when Adam and Eve sinned in the Garden. Therefore, He had to learn from these events and develop a remedy to hopefully resolve them. This position absolves God from any wrongdoing, lest someone blame Him for creating or even allowing sin to enter the world. This system requires a denial of the sovereignty of God, a heretical position that preserves man's rabid commitment to self-determination by making man, not God, the one ultimately in charge of a person's destiny.

Others in the class held a similar position but with a slight twist. They held the classic *Arminian* position that is by far the most popular default opinion among Christians today.

They argued that God did not *ordain* or in any way *cause* sin to come into existence and is therefore not responsible for it; He only responded to the situation when it arose. "After all," they would contend, "if God were in control, man could not be held morally responsible for sin." They believe that while God knew what was happening, He chose not to exercise His power to stop it.

The obvious priority of this position is to preserve the freedom of the human will to make moral choices, which, in their mind, clears God of any blame for causing evil to enter the world while at the same time provides the only legitimate way God could hold man morally accountable for his rebellion. By making God contingent on man's free choices, He also provides the necessary life context for human beings to learn from their mistakes through their sins, bad choices, and especially the suffering and evil they experience. In so doing, it is believed, they learn to truly love and trust God as He *hopes* they will, but cannot guarantee.

While I believe both *Process Theology* and the various flavors of *Arminianism* to be unbiblical positions, they certainly seem plausible on the surface to explain the origin of sin, God's role in evil and suffering, and so many other sticky issues related to soteriology. As a young man, I held to *Arminianism* (though I didn't know that was what it was called early on) because it fit my conception of the kind of God I wanted. I was unable to see from Scripture how human free will and divine determination are complementary and therefore compatible in the purposes of God.

Yet I would humbly assert that it is clear from Scripture that depraved human nature is incapable of obeying God and cannot do so apart from divine intervention. Because of his corrupt nature, man is a slave to sin and will relish it apart from regenerating grace (soteriological concepts beyond the purview of this book). But as we consider God's role in evil and suffering, *we must not only accept the compatibility of God's sovereignty and man's responsibility, but also the compatibility of God's infinite love and goodness even in the presence of evil.*

The problem with the popular positions of the people in the aforementioned Sunday School class, reflective of the majority of Christendom, is that they cannot be reconciled with the sovereign God of the Bible. They are at loggerheads with His revelation of Himself. To imply that God values man's will more than His own reduces Him to being little more than man's servant whose will is contingent upon the choices of mere human beings, notwithstanding the inscrutable mystery and compatibility between God's sovereignty and man's responsibility—that both propositions are equally true simultaneously. The biblical record makes it clear (as I will attempt to demonstrate from Scripture) that *God has indeed ordained to allow evil to exist in His created order as an integral part of His plan and purpose to glorify Himself.* But even in His permissive providence, He retains His sovereign control and inherent goodness.

If we make the Creator subservient to His creation by denying His sovereignty over all things that exist, we disregard His revelation of himself as the One who, "[declares] the end from the beginning, and from ancient times things which have not been done, saying, 'My purpose will be established, and I will accomplish all My good pleasure'" (Isa. 46:10). Whether we like it or even believe it, the God of the Bible reigns supreme over His creation as the One who "works all things after the counsel of His will" (Eph. 1:11). He is God, and we are not. This introduces the third and least popular theological system, the *Reformed* position, anchored in a biblical soteriology (doctrine of salvation).

3

The Reformed Position

From the outset, in order to understand the *Reformed* position, and therefore be faithful to Scripture with respect to God's role in tragedies and atrocities, it is crucial to underscore some fundamental doctrines pertaining to God's *sovereignty*, *omniscience*, and the *origin of sin*. It is primarily a misunderstanding—or in many cases the outright rejection—of these biblical doctrines that causes so many people to either *attack* or *rescue* the character of God for ordaining the existence of evil and suffering. So let's examine these briefly in order to lay a proper theological foundation upon which we can build a solid superstructure able to withstand the inevitable storms of doubt and bewilderment that can topple our faith and rob God of the glory He deserves.

Sovereignty

First, consider God's sovereignty: *His absolute rule and authority over all things*. Like perhaps no other doctrine, this is the greatest source of comfort to the redeemed when experiencing some profound heartache and loss. Knowing God is fully *aware of* and *in charge of* all that happens instantly delegitimizes thoughts of abandonment, indifference, or randomness (though in our humanness, we are bound to *feel* otherwise). Nothing catches Him by surprise, including evil and suffering. Indeed, He is a *sovereign*, not a *contingent*, God. There is therefore nothing in our life He has not *ordained to accomplish, allow*, or *understand completely*, including the sufferings, tragedies, and atrocities we experience. His character is in no need of *rescue*, nor is it even remotely worthy of *attack*.

Regarding His *sovereignty*, we must remember that he is the One who, "[declares] the end from the beginning, and from ancient times things which have not been done, saying, 'My purpose will be established, and I will accomplish all My good pleasure'" (Isa. 46:10). There is nothing man can do to escape His influence: "The mind of man plans his way, but the Lord directs his steps" (Prov. 16:9; cf. Jer. 10:23). Daniel described God as the One who "does according to His will in the host of heaven and among the inhabitants of earth; and no one can ward off His hand or say to Him, 'What have You done?'" (4:35; cf. Ps. 135:6). In these and many other verses, God leaves no doubt that He reigns in absolute sovereignty over His creation as the One who "works all things after the counsel of His will" (Eph. 1:11). This also speaks to the *immensity* of God (that He fills all space and transcends it) and the *omnipresence* of God (that His entire being is present with every point of space)—subjects beyond the scope of this discussion, but inextricably bound to it (see Gen. 14:19, 22; Deut. 10:14; 1 Kings 8:27; 2 Chron. 2:6; Isa. 66:1; Ps. 139:7-10; Jer. 23:23-24; Acts 7:48-49; 17:27-28; Col. 1:16; Rev. 10:6).

What a comforting truth to know that no matter how bad our circumstance, how hopeless our condition, how unfair our plight, God is ultimately in absolute rule and authority over all things and His purposes for our eternal welfare and His ineffable majesty cannot be thwarted.

Omniscience

Regarding His *omniscience*, we can also find comfort knowing, "The Lord looks from heaven; He sees all the sons of men; from His dwelling place He looks out on all the inhabitants of the earth, He who fashions the hearts of them all, He who understands all their works" (Ps. 33:13-15). His knowledge is infinitely perfect and requires no further information (Isa. 40:13-14; Rom. 11:34); it precedes all things outside of Himself and is never obtained from anything that exists outside Himself (Rom. 8:29; 1 Cor. 2:7; Eph. 1:4-5; 2 Tim. 1:9). For this reason, in utter awe David described how God knew the minutest details of his life (Ps. 139:1-6). In Psalm 147 the Lord is praised as the One who heals the brokenhearted; the One who "counts the number of the stars; He gives names to all of them. Great is the Lord and abundant in strength; His understanding is infinite" (v. 4).

There is nothing man can think or do that escapes His notice, including *tragedies* and *atrocities*, "For the ways of a man are before the eyes of the Lord, and He watches all his paths" (Prov. 5:21). Indeed, "The eyes of the Lord are in every place, watching the evil and the good" (Prov. 15:3). "His understanding is inscrutable" (Isa. 40:28); "There is no creature hidden from His sight, but all things are open and laid bare to the eyes of Him with whom we have to do" (Heb. 4:13); "He knows everything" (1 John 3:19).

While this fallen world is plagued by every imaginable form of evil and "the sufferings of Christ are ours in abundance" (2 Cor. 1:5), we can find relief knowing His sanctifying purposes are always at work in our lives and nothing happens outside the sphere of His ultimate control and intimate awareness. For this reason, Paul exhorts us to "exult in our tribulations" (Rom. 5:3)—not merely rejoice in spite of them or resign ourselves to them and somehow choose to be happy; not even rejoice in the midst of them, though that is important. What he is saying is that we are to exult *because* of our tribulations, *on account* of them! And he goes on to tell us why: "knowing that tribulation brings about perseverance; and perseverance, proven character; and proven character, hope; and hope does not disappoint, because the love of God has been poured out within our hearts through the Holy Spirit who was given to us" (Rom. 5:3-5). He obviously understood that God ordains and oversees our afflictions for our good and His glory, though we seldom see it at the time.

To be sure, it requires a special measure of Spirit-empowered faith to trust God in the fires of affliction, knowing that all that is burned off is our dross. But only then can we have the confidence to say with Job, "When He has tried me, I shall come forth as gold" (Job 23:10). No saint will be able to survive the tragedies and atrocities of life unless he or she understands and fully rejoices in the weighty truth that *authentic faith must and will be tested by fire* (1 Peter 1:7). An untested faith is a dubious faith, and an untried commitment is an unreliable commitment. Therefore, through His *sovereignty* and *omniscience* He accomplishes His glorious purposes in the lives of those He loves, conforming us into the likeness of Christ for our good and His glory.

4

God's Glory and the Origin of Sin

The ability to not only survive evil and suffering, but to actually transcend its effects upon the soul, also requires a biblical understanding of the *origin of sin*—a doctrine that was totally foreign to the Sunday School class, and most evangelicals today.

Despite the prevailing ignorance within the ranks of modern evangelicalism, Scripture clearly teaches that, although God ordained and decreed sin to enter His perfect universe through the voluntary choices of moral creatures, it is a supreme blasphemy to consider God the *author* or *cause* of sin. Because God is infinitely holy (Lev. 11:44,45), utterly bereft of any form of unrighteousness (Deut. 32:4; Ps. 92:15), He cannot act wickedly (Job 34:10). Habakkuk said of the Lord, "Your eyes are too pure to approve evil and You can not look on wickedness with favor" (Hab. 1:13). Scripture also reveals that

God cannot be tempted by evil or solicit anyone to do evil. This is also affirmed in James 1:13: "Let no one say when he is tempted, 'I am being tempted by God'; for God cannot be tempted by evil, and He Himself does not tempt anyone." With confidence we can therefore join the psalmist and declare, "The judgments of the Lord are true; they are righteous altogether" (Ps. 19:19).

We can therefore conclude: *While our holy God is never the cause of sin, He does bring it about indirectly through the willing, voluntary actions of moral creatures.* This is evident in God's testimony of Himself when he said, "I form the light, and create darkness: I make peace, and create evil: I the Lord do all these things" (Isa. 45:7, KJV). Culver offers this helpful insight:

> This language seems to assign the natural evils mentioned to God's direct agency. It is, however, only a manner of speaking. It was clearly understood by the ones for whom the Bible was first written to apply to God's permissive providence operating through second causes toward certain ends which God's wisdom appoints.[6]

God's "permissive providence operating through second causes" would include not only the evil propensity in Satan and the angelic beings, but also the actual decree that they would eventually rebel. Although all the angelic beings were created originally "very good" (Gen. 1:31), the New Testament makes it clear that Satan was a "murderer from the beginning" and is "the father of lies" (John 8:44).

This means that at some time subsequent to his creation, he, along with other angels, chose to sin and rebel against God (Isa. 14:12-15; cf. 2 Peter 2:4; Jude 6; Rev. 12:4). While in the permissive providence of God He allowed the "ancient serpent" (Rev. 12:9) to enter His original paradise, He also makes it clear that that same serpent and his minions will not be allowed in the final paradise (Rev. 21:27). So none of this caught God by surprise. He retains ultimate control to accomplish His eternal purposes. For this reason, He says of Himself, "I am God, and there is none like me, declaring the end from the beginning and from ancient times things not yet done" (Isa. 46:9c-10).

John also tells us that "the devil has sinned from the beginning," referring to the first time he rebelled against God. But he goes on to add that "the Son of God appeared for this purpose, to destroy the works of the devil" (1 John 3:8). This indicates that even the devil's diabolical works had to have been divinely ordained because Christ was "delivered up by the predetermined plan and foreknowledge of

God" (Acts 2:23). Satan's original rebellion against God, his temptation of Eve in the garden, his temptation of Christ, his future empowerment of the Antichrist, his notorious opposition to the work of God, all had to have been known by an omniscient God who also ordained them by His uninfluenced will. To say otherwise would deny His right and claim to sovereignty and cause these texts to beg for relevance.

We can therefore reason that God's elective, eternal purposes were decreed and set into motion before creation. This would include the Lord's incarnation and atoning work that defeated Satan and sin. Here again we see that *He ordained to allow evil to enter His perfect universe through the voluntary choices of moral creatures in order to dramatically display His glory through His holiness, wrath, mercy, grace, love and power.* Indeed, all of His elective purposes were ordained "from all eternity" (2 Tim. 1:9; Titus 1:2), literally, "before time began," which would, by implication, include His divine decree for Satan to rebel, Adam and Eve to sin, and, by imputation, all men to sin in Adam, thus requiring "the Lamb [to be] slain from the foundation of the world" (Rev. 13:8).

That God brought about evil to accomplish His glorious purposes was well understood by His covenant people in the Old Testament. We see this in their repentance when in utmost contrition they cried out to God and said, "Why, O Lord, do You cause us to stray from Your ways and harden our heart from fearing You?" (Isa. 63:17). As stated earlier, speaking through Isaiah, the Lord said, "I am the Lord, there is no other. Besides Me there is no God . . . The One forming light and creating darkness, causing well-being and creating calamity; I am the Lord who does all these" (Isa. 45:6-7). Likewise, the prophet Jeremiah lamented, "Is it not from the mouth of the Most High that both good and ill go forth?" (Lam. 3:38).

Solomon reminds us that, "the Lord has made all things for Himself, even the wicked for the day of evil." Hannah praised God's sovereignty—even over evil—when she prayed, "The Lord kills and makes alive; He brings down to Sheol and raises up. The Lord makes poor and rich; He brings low, He also exalts" (1 Sam. 2:6-7). The prophet Amos also declared, "If a calamity occurs in a city has not the Lord done it?" (Amos 3:6).

We never know for sure what God may be up to when suffering as a result of evil afflicts us in some painful and unexpected way. We can never know God's secret will (Deut. 29:29); we can only submit to it, confident that it comes from the hand of a loving Father. We have trials because we need them, and we have no more of them than we are in need of.

I'm sure Joseph felt confused when his brothers captured him and sold him into slavery—a great example of God's providence orchestrating evil through the choices of sinful individuals. The essence of this doctrinal truth can be seen when Joseph forgave the sinful acts of his brothers and said, "As for you, you meant evil against me, but God meant it for good in order to bring about this present result, to preserve many people alive" (Gen. 50:20).

Similarly, when Israel conquered the exceedingly wicked people of Canaan, in Joshua 11 we read, "Joshua waged war a long time with all these kings. There was not a city which made peace with the sons of Israel except the Hivites living in Gibeon; they took them all in battle. *For it was of the Lord to harden their hearts*, to meet Israel in battle in order that he might utterly destroy them, that they might receive no mercy, but that he might destroy them, just as the Lord had commanded Moses" (vv. 18-20; emphasis added).

God's sovereign rule over the affairs of men by indirectly bringing about sin through their choices is also evident in the account of Exodus when "The Lord said to Moses, 'When you go back to Egypt see that you perform before Pharaoh all the wonders which I have put in your power; but I will harden his heart so that he will not let the people go'" (Ex. 4:21); then later God told Moses, "But I will harden Pharaoh's heart that I may multiply My signs and My wonders in the land of Egypt" (7:3; cf. 9:16; 14:17).

When God judged David for his sin, he also brought about evil through the willing actions of David's family. There we see God using sin to punish sin. We read of this in 1 Samuel: "Thus says the LORD, 'Behold, I will raise up evil against you from your own household; I will even take your wives before your eyes and give them to your companion, and he will lie with your wives in broad daylight. Indeed you did it secretly, but I will do this thing before all Israel, and under the sun'" (1 Sam. 12:11-12). This was later fulfilled during Absalom's rebellion when he publicly violated David's royal concubines as an act of total domination (16:21, 22), thus proving this was God's work.

God also raised up the wicked Chaldeans to punish Israel, but then punished the Chaldeans for what they did to Israel (Hab. 1:6-11). Though God's providence may seem impulsive, vicious, and even unfair to our fallen and finite mind, nevertheless this theme is repeated over and over in the Old Testament. *While God never directly acts wickedly, nor does*

He take pleasure in evil, He indirectly brings it about through individuals who voluntarily exercise their own will and are thereby held accountable for their actions.

This is apparent in 2 Samuel 24:1 where we read that "the anger of the Lord burned against Israel, and it incited David against them to say, 'Go, number Israel and Judah.'" Then later, after the census had been taken, David confessed what God had incited him to do was sin (v. 10). It is fascinating to note that *even though the Lord incited David to sin* (by using Satan to achieve his purposes) — see 1 Chr. 21:1 — *David was clearly held responsible for his actions*.

With respect to God's judgment upon the wicked, which can result in the most horrifying atrocities, God does not merely allow, but He actively superintends. By calling Nebuchadnezzar "the servant of God," (2 Sam. 12:12), Jeremiah stated that the unimaginable cruelties perpetrated upon Judea by the Chaldeans were clearly a work of God. Scripture is filled with examples of how divine judgment has been meted out upon countless people groups and will continue until "He has put all things in subjection under His feet" (1 Cor. 15:27).

Speaking of Satan's power to exert his authority to rule over those who reject the truth, the apostle Paul says "the god of this world has blinded the minds of the unbelieving so that they might not see the light of the gospel of the glory of Christ" (2 Cor. 4:4). Obviously this could not happen apart from God sending deceptive errors that cause those who "will not endure sound doctrine" to "turn away their ears from the truth, and . . . turn aside to myths" (2 Tim. 4:3-4). Calvin summarizes this well when he says,

> . . . nothing can be clearer than the many passages which declare, that he blinds the minds of men, and smites them with giddiness, intoxicates them with a spirit of stupor, renders them infatuated, and hardens their hearts. Even these expressions many would confine to permissions as if, by deserting the reprobate, he allowed them to be blinded by Satan. But since the Holy Spirit distinctly says, that the blindness and infatuation are inflicted by the just judgment of God, the solution is altogether inadmissible.[7]

Calvin went on to add this:

> The sum of the whole is this—since the will of God is said to be the cause of all things, all the counsels and actions of men must be held to be governed by his providence; so that he not only exerts his power in the elect, who are guided by the Holy Spirit, but also forces the reprobate to do him service.[8]

Nowhere is this more evident than the greatest tragedy and atrocity ever committed in the history of the world—the crucifixion of the sinless Savior, the Lord Jesus Christ.

5

The Tragedy and Atrocity of the Crucifixion of Christ

Reflecting once again upon my short conversation with the Sunday School class, it was obvious to each of them that indeed the crucifixion of Christ was the greatest of all evils; that God was more, not less, glorified because of it and, as a result, sinners are able to experience more, not less, happiness. But several in the class struggled, and understandably so, with the idea of God's providential working in the lives of evil men who, by His sovereign decree, independently chose by their own free will to act wickedly in participating in heinous acts. Most indicated that they had never thought about it that way.

Obviously, none of what happened caught God by surprise nor were the choices of those wicked men a violation of His sovereign will. This was evident in the prayer of Peter and John when they stated, "For truly in this city there were gathered together against Your holy servant Jesus, whom You anointed, both Herod and Pontius Pilate, along with the Gentiles and the peoples of Israel, *to do whatever Your hand and Your purpose predestined to occur*" (Acts 4:27, emphasis added).

Every Christian would do well to remember that the Father's wrath of judgment against sin was poured out upon His Son and our substitute, Jesus Christ. Notwithstanding the responsibility of wicked men who cried out for Him to be crucified, Peter made it clear that God ordained His murder when he said, "this Man, delivered up by the *predetermined plan* and *foreknowledge of God*, you nailed to a cross by the hands of godless men and put Him to death" (Acts 2:23, emphasis added).

What an amazing concept: *Jesus willingly chose to suffer and die on a cross because God ordained Him to do so*. He was delivered up by the "predetermined plan." The word *predetermined* is the Greek word *horizo*, meaning "to mark out a boundary beforehand," from which we get our English word horizon. The word *plan* translates the Greek word *boule* used in Scripture to describe God's will of purpose; that which He has designed, ordained, or decreed in eternity past. Sometimes this is referred to as His decretive or sovereign will. So Peter is literally saying that *our sovereign God decreed that Jesus would die on the cross; it was His predetermined plan.*

Furthermore, he attributes His sacrificial death to the "foreknowledge of God." The word *foreknowledge* is the Greek word *prognosis* meaning "to foreordain"—a meaning that far exceeds the English concept of merely knowing something ahead of time. Moreover, grammatically speaking, since the term is in the instrumental dative case, it must be understood that Peter was actually saying, "It was God's foreknowledge (foreordination) that was *the sole cause or the means by which* the men nailed Him to a cross." Stated simply, *Jesus did exactly what God ordained Him to do, yet those who called for His death and hung Him on the tree were responsible for His murder.* Here again we see not only the mysterious convergence of God's sovereignty and man's responsibility, but also God deliberately ordaining an evil event to exist as a part of His plan and purpose to glorify Himself—the greatest act of evil in all of history: *the murder of Jesus Christ.*

Unlike the misguided musings of the Sunday School class, the testimony of Scripture plainly reveals that God is indeed sovereign over His creation. And though He is never responsible for sin,

He does bring it about through the voluntary choices of men and He holds them accountable for their actions. Moreover, not only is God removed from actually doing evil, *but never do we find an instance in Scripture of any act of evil surprising God and requiring Him to react with a "Plan B."*

In light of all this, it is obvious that no example can be found supporting the *Arminian* notion that God merely allowed the possibility for evil to exist in order to give His creatures freedom of choice, thereby guaranteeing that man's choices would always be meaningful, as some would suggest. Instead, we see a sovereign God orchestrating His universe through the use of both good and evil.

6

God's Role in Israel's Unbelief

The example of Israel's unbelief found in Romans 9 adds further insight into the question of how God ordained evil to accomplish His purposes and did so without impugning His character. After proclaiming the marvels of justification by faith, Paul interrupted his doctrinal treatise with chapters 9-11 to clarify some important truths pertaining to his fellow Jews and God's ultimate plan for Israel. No doubt he had already encountered an angry response from unbelieving Jews who were profoundly offended by the gospel message where, in their minds, their supposed Messiah not only rejected their traditions and system of works righteousness as a means of salvation, but, worse yet, it offered salvation to the Gentiles. Their anger was further exacerbated by His scathing denunciation of their hypocritical legalism and the sham of their rabbinic traditions.

For them, the gospel of Jesus Christ was an anti-Jewish conspiracy. They were convinced that simply because they were the physical descendants of Abraham, they were the heirs of promise and guaranteed recipients of divine favor. The idea of justification by grace alone through faith alone shattered their entire system. They could not fathom how the blood of Christ could ratify a New Covenant and replace the Old Covenant. It was blasphemy to think that anything could replace the Law. For them, both Jesus and the apostle Paul were traitors and blasphemers. Furthermore, it was beyond their ability to understand how the gospel could possibly be "the power of God for salvation to everyone who believes, to the Jew first and also to the Greek" (Rom. 1:16). How could this be true given the rampant unbelief among the Jewish people and the vile character of the Gentiles?

Having undoubtedly experienced the vitriol of his countrymen, and anticipating even more when those in Rome read his letter, the loving apostle spends three chapters explaining the truth of God's redemptive plan as it related to them. He longed to see them come to a saving knowledge of the truth through repentant faith, saying, "I am telling the truth in Christ, I am not lying, my conscience bearing me witness in the Holy Spirit, that I have great sorrow and unceasing grief in my heart. For I could wish that I myself were accursed, separated from Christ for the sake of my brethren, my kinsmen according to the flesh" (Rom. 9:1-3).

It is in the context of this fascinating discourse we discover a series of examples of divine sovereignty, especially as it relates to our topic of God's role in ordaining evil and sin. Citing God's uninfluenced and unmerited choice to bless Isaac over Ishmael (vv. 7-10) and Jacob over Esau (vv. 11-13), Paul demonstrates that *God chooses whom He will to be His spiritual children.* Then, anticipating the human assertion that God is unfair in His sovereign choice of some and not all, he defends God's fairness and extols His mercy by recalling his dealings with Moses and the golden calf worshippers (v.19). Although God would have been justified in killing them all, He instead chose to only kill "twenty-four thousand" (Num. 25:9).

His argument continued by reminding them of God's mighty act of deliverance when He rescued Israel from the Egyptians. In this account we see yet another example of God's just and sovereign rule even though He hardened the hearts of some, as seen in His dealing with Moses versus Pharaoh (vv. 17-18). And finally, in anticipation of the inevitable resentment of the sovereignty of God in salvation by carnal minds that would impose upon Him their standard of justice, the Holy Spirit speaks through His servant and declares emphatically in the inspired text:

> So then He has mercy on whom he desires, and He hardens whom He desires. You will say to me then, "Why does He still find fault? For who resists His will?" On the contrary, who are you, O man, who answers back to God? The thing molded will not say to the molder, "Why did you make me like this," will it? Or does not the potter have a right over the clay, to make from the same lump one vessel for honorable use, and another for common use? What if God, although willing to demonstrate His wrath and to make His power known, endured with much patience vessels of wrath prepared for destruction? And He did so in order that He might make known the riches of His glory upon vessels of mercy, which He prepared beforehand for glory, even us, whom He also called, not from among Jews only, but also from among Gentiles (Rom. 9:18-24).

Here again we see the divine prerogative to act as He will toward His creation and to do so with absolute righteousness. He is the potter; we are the clay—indeed, we are but dust. What insolence to protest His sovereignty yet demand it for ourselves.

What arrogant foolishness to cry, "Foul! Unfair! What gives You the right to rule and whimsically save some and not all? What justice is there in such limited selection?" But, as we will discover, His Word is clear: *Nothing He does is capricious or cruel, but always perfectly just and part of His flawless plan to bring eternal glory to Himself.*

Therefore, Paul argues that for an ignorant, self-willed human being to sit in judgment over God and question the wisdom and fairness of His sovereign choices is as absurd as a clay pot demanding an explanation from its creator as to why he made it the way he did (vv. 20-21). Paul is simply saying, "To even question God is ludicrous!" Obviously, a clay pot has no ability whatsoever to reason and is infinitely inferior to the potter who made it—a perfect analogy exposing the boundless chasm between God and man, and therefore the ridiculous basis of charging God with being unfair in His choice of some and not all.

7

Three Reasons God Ordained to Allow Evil

It is important to point out that Paul's purpose in this passage is not to definitively explain the inscrutable mysteries of sovereign election and man's responsibility (developed more fully in Romans 10 and 11), or the sacred harmony between His justice and righteousness, or even the origin of sin, but to clarify God's purposes for Israel in her rejection of Jesus Christ. Yet, by demonstrating that God's dealings with man are fair, we discover some fascinating insights relevant to our discussion of God's purposes in ordaining sin to invade His perfect universe through His permissive providence. The apostle Paul gives us great insight into this vast mystery when he says:

What if God, although willing to demonstrate His wrath and to make His power known, endured with much patience vessels of wrath prepared for destruction? And *He did so* to make known the riches of His glory upon vessels of mercy, which He prepared beforehand for glory, *even* us, whom He also called, not from among Jews only, but also from among Gentiles (Rom. 9:22-24).

Here we learn of at least three reasons God gives for ordaining to allow evil to exist in His perfect universe:

- to demonstrate His wrath;
- to make His power known;
- to make known the riches of His glory on vessels of mercy.

Let's look more closely at each one, because here we will discover that God has indeed *ordained to allow evil to enter His perfect universe through the voluntary choices of moral creatures in order to dramatically display His glory through His holiness, wrath, mercy, grace, love and power.*

To Demonstrate His Wrath

The first of these insights emerges from Paul's rhetorical question, "What if God, although willing to demonstrate His wrath and to make His power known, endured with much patience vessels of wrath prepared for destruction?" (v. 22). His use of the Greek word *thelo* translated "willing" is a strong term that far exceeds our English notion of casual compliance or consent. Rather, it denotes a resolute, unyielding, deliberate choice. He did this for the same reason He does everything: *because He is an infinitely holy God who fully intends to put His eternal glory on display!* This is precisely why the Holy Spirit inspired Paul to use the example of God's purposes with Pharaoh (and all who oppose Him) at the end of verse 17: "For this very purpose I raised you up, to demonstrate My power in you, and that My name might be proclaimed throughout the whole earth."

In light of this we must ask, "Why did He resolutely determine to endure 'with much patience vessels of wrath prepared for destruction?'" (v. 22b). First he answers, *"To demonstrate His wrath"* (v. 22a; emphasis added). Since God's ultimate goal in all He does is to bring glory to Himself, we can reason from this text that He not only ordained sin to enter the world, but chose to endure the wickedness of men until a day of ultimate reckoning when "the wrath of God comes upon the sons of disobedience" (Eph. 5:6: cf. John 3:36).

Here the apostle, writing under the inspiration of the Holy Spirit, reveals how God's mercy will continue to *endure* until the last of the pre-kingdom judgments have been executed, culminating in unimaginable fury when our Lord Christ returns "and treads the wine press of the fierce wrath of God, the Almighty" (Rev. 19:15). Then, in transcendent glory, "the kingdom of the world [will become] the kingdom of our Lord, and of His Christ; and He will reign forever and ever" (Rev. 11:15). The glory of such a display of divine retribution exceeds the limits of language and imagination. This will be a spectacle of sheer majesty and supernatural power, all part of His eternal plan to glorify Himself, as Solomon made evident in his inspired declaration where he said, "The LORD has made everything for its own purpose, even the wicked for the day of evil" (Prov. 16:4).

Think of the immense joy when some great evil is put down and justice is finally served. Who can forget the day United States troops dragged the Iraqi despot Saddam Hussein from a hole in the ground? The civilized world erupted in celebration. Then later we witnessed his public hanging, and again people danced in the streets with joy. Remember the elation when the US Navy Seals killed the mass murderer Osama Bin Laden? Whenever a wicked fiend is finally punished, and the oppressed vindicated, there is great happiness among the people, and honor bestowed upon the victor.

The same will be true when sin, Satan, and death—although defeated at the cross—will one day be vanquished forever. For this reason, God is glorified in His wrath. At Christ's second coming, divine justice will be served upon the nations (Rev. 19:15,16). His holiness will be vindicated as He takes vengeance upon His enemies (Deut. 32:41). His victory will also be our victory as we share in the undeserved prize of eternal glory, for we are His "children, heirs also, heirs of God and fellow heirs with Christ" (Rom. 8:17; cf. Col. 1:12).

In God's wrath we also see an unrivaled contrast between His mercy (Deut. 32:35, 36) and the mind-boggling disparity between heaven and hell. In addition to the numerous instances of divine judgment manifested through redemptive history and the ultimate wrath of eternal hell, both the Old and New Testaments describe a period of eschatological wrath that will occur during a time of unprecedented worldwide tribulation just prior to the unveiling of Jesus Christ when He returns in majestic glory as King of kings and Lord of lords to establish His promised Messianic Kingdom.

The Bible speaks of this as a time when the wicked will cry out "to the mountains and to the rocks, 'Fall on us and hide us from the presence of Him who sits on the throne, and from the wrath of the Lamb; for the great day of their wrath has come, and who is able to stand?'" (Rev. 6:16, 17). Can there be a more stunning display of God's glory? So indeed, the existence of sin and evil provides the perfect context in which God will demonstrate His holiness through the display of His wrath, and by contrast, the glory of His grace toward those who believe.

To Make His Power Known

Paul's rhetorical question offers a second reason why God allowed sin to invade his universe: "*to make His power known*" (v. 22; emphasis added). Biblical illustrations abound in this regard. Think how God's power was made known when He poured out His wrath upon the Egyptians who dared to trifle with the God of Israel by pursuing His people. After the sons of Israel walked on dry land through the midst of the sea "and the waters were like a wall to them on their right hand and on their left"

(Ex. 14:29), the Lord covered the pursuing Egyptian chariots and horseman with the waters (v. 28). Then we read, "Thus the Lord saved Israel that day from the hand of the Egyptians, and Israel saw the Egyptians dead on the seashore. When Israel saw the great power which the Lord had used against the Egyptians, the people feared the Lord, and they believed in the Lord and in His servant Moses" (vv. 30, 31). Astounded by the irresistible power of divine wrath, Moses and the sons of Israel then burst into song (Ex. 15:1-18).

In His revelation, the Lord Jesus Christ discloses similar demonstrations of divine wrath being poured out upon this sin-cursed earth just prior to His return (Rev. 6-19). The very thought of such catastrophic violence causes us to tremble. The sheer magnitude of His power is incomprehensible and inconceivably glorious. Even as His glory was manifested in creation, it will also be revealed again in His re-creation when "the day of the Lord will come like a thief, in which the heavens will pass away with a roar and the elements will be destroyed with intense heat, and the earth and its works will be burned up" (1 Peter 3:10). Peter then adds, "But according to His promise we are looking for new heavens and a new earth, in which righteousness dwells" (v. 13). Language is not capable of expressing the kind of power and authority this would require, nor could words possibly convey the magnificent honor this will bring to our Lord Christ.

Nevertheless, some will still argue that God is unfair in His sovereign rule over the affairs of men, especially in light of his wrath being reserved for "vessels of wrath prepared for destruction" (v. 22c). But it is important to remember that while it is true that God has ordained sin to be in the world, it is equally true that *man is the one who voluntarily chooses to act wickedly.* The blame cannot be placed upon God, but man. That this is true is evident in the Greek verb *katartizo* rendered "prepared" (v. 22c). Grammatically we see that this verb is in the passive voice, meaning God is not the subject doing the preparing, but rather it is the willful disobedience of sinful man. All who refuse to embrace His gift of grace through faith are responsible for their rebellion and are therefore *preparing themselves* for the wrath to come. All who cry out for mercy will receive it; those who reject it will be judged. They are therefore described as "vessels of wrath prepared for destruction" (v. 22c).

Surely His power *will* be made known in the wrath of His indignation upon those who have willfully chosen not to believe and obey. Yet we beg God to spare them. To this end we pray, even as

Paul prayed for his fellow countrymen, "my heart's desire and prayer to God for Israel is that they may be saved" (Rom. 10:1).

To Make Known the Riches of His Glory on Vessels of Mercy

Paul goes on to describe yet a third reason God ordained sin: "*He did so to make known the riches of His glory upon vessels of mercy*, which He prepared beforehand for glory, even us, whom he also called, not from among Jews only, but also from among Gentiles" (Rom. 9:23, 24, emphasis added). Here we are reminded again of God's love for those whom He has called to Himself. A vessel is not a fountain, but a container, and the One who fashioned it must fill it up. How thankful we can be that we have received *mercy* instead of the *wrath of justice* we deserve.

Here again we see that by allowing sin in the world, God provided an opportunity to glorify Himself not only in His wrath and power, but also in the *redemption of His people* (v. 23). What a magnificent reality for all who have been saved by His grace. He saved us "to make known the riches of His glory"—and to think that *we* are "vessels of mercy, which He prepared beforehand for glory"

(v. 23c). I cannot think of a more humbling and spiritually motivating truth than this: *our salvation was part of His sovereign plan to glorify Himself, determined and decreed in eternity past* (Eph. 1:3-14; cf. 2 Tim. 1:9; Titus 1:1, 2). For this reason Paul rejoiced in his sufferings and in the privilege of preaching the "word of God . . . to His saints, to whom God willed to make known what is the riches of the glory of this mystery among the Gentiles, which is Christ in you, the hope of glory" (Col. 1:25-27). May this be our sincere testimony as well.

8

All Things for Good

As I reflect upon the countless times as a pastor that I have had the privilege of comforting those in great distress, and when I consider the multiple sorrows I have experienced personally, I realize that these great truths regarding God's perfections and purposes in evil and suffering are always the Spirit-empowered remedy for every sickness of the soul and every loss of the heart. Emboldened and encouraged by these truths, my faith is fortified and I can honestly say that when the night is the darkest, God's presence is the brightest. This was David's testimony when surrounded by great terror testified,

> But as for me, I trust in You, O Lord, I say, "You are my God." My times are in Your hand; Deliver me from the hand of my enemies, and from those who persecute me, Make Your face to shine upon Your servant; Save me in Your lovingkindness. . . How great is Your goodness, which You have stored up

for those who fear You, which You have wrought for those who take refuge in You"
(Psalm 31: 14-16, 19).

To know that God is always up to something in our life is utterly incomprehensible. But He is. Even when life hurts and we don't want to go on. And in those times of hopelessness and helplessness, the rich truths that emerge from Paul's familiar words in Romans 8:28 take on new meaning: "And we know that God causes all things to work together for good to those who love God, to those who are called according to His purpose." Knowing that in His sweet providence He is orchestrating every temptation, every sorrow, even every sin, to accomplish His purposes in our life both now and for eternity, is a reality that should cause our troubled soul to find peace even in the greatest tempest.

The wise and godly Puritan, Thomas Watson, unpacks this great text in ways that I have personally found most helpful in his book, *All Things for Good*. I offer but a sample for your benefit. He states,

> If all things work for good, hence learn that there is a providence. Things do not work of themselves, but God sets them working for good. God is the great Disposer of all events and issues. He sets everything working. "His kingdom ruleth over

all" (Psalm 103.19). It is meant of His providential kingdom. Things in the world are not governed by second causes, by the counsels of men, by the stars and planets, but by divine providence. Providence is the queen and governess of the world. There are three things in providence: God's foreknowing, God's determining, and God's directing all things to their periods and events. Whatever things do work in the world, God sets them a working. [9]

He goes on to offer moving reminders of the many ways we can witness the providences of God at work in our lives, perhaps unwittingly; evoking within us the breathless adoration He deserves. He says,

> See here the wisdom of God, who can make the worst things imaginable turn to the good of the saints. He can by a divine chemistry extract gold out of dross. "Oh the depth of the wisdom of God!" (Rom. 11.33). It is God's great design to set forth the wonder of His wisdom. The Lord made Joseph's prison a step to preferment. There was no way for Jonah to be saved, but by being swallowed up. God suffered the Egyptians to hate Israel (Psalm 106.41), and this was the means of their deliverance. The apostle Paul was bound with a chain, and that chain which did bind him was the means of enlarging the gospel (Phil. 1.12). God enriches by impoverishing; He causes the augmenta-

tion of grace by the diminution of an estate. When the creature goes further from us, it is that Christ may come nearer to us. God works strangely. He brings order out of confusion, harmony out of discord. He frequently makes use of unjust men to do that which is just. "He is wise in heart" (Job 9.4). He can reap His glory out of men's fury (Psalm 76.10). Either the wicked shall not do the hurt that they intend, or they shall do the good which they do not intend. God often helps when there is least hope, and saves His people in that way which they think will destroy. He made use of the high-priest's malice and Judas' treason to redeem the world. Through indiscreet passion, we are apt to find fault with things that happen; which is as if an illiterate man should censure philosophy, or a blind man find fault with the work in a landscape. "Vain man would be wise" (Job 11.12). Silly animals will be taxing Providence, and calling the wisdom of God to the bar of reason. God's ways are "past finding out" (Rom. 11.33). They are rather to be admired than fathomed. There is never a providence of God, but has either a mercy or a wonder in it. How stupendous and infinite is that wisdom, that makes the most adverse dispensations work for the good of His children![10]

Those who truly love God can find some measure of comfort even when their emotional knees buckle under the crushing weight of suffering knowing that "God causes all things to work together for good to those who love God, to those who are called according to His purpose" (Rom. 8:28). But none of us is immune to soul-crushing despair. Even our Savior needed an angel from heaven to strengthen Him. "And being in agony He was praying very fervently; and His sweat became like drops of blood, falling down upon the ground" (Luke 22:44). So *when*, not *if*, we find ourselves despairing of life itself, feeling as though God has abandoned us in our pain and we are left to our own resources, there is no shame in crying aloud with the Psalmist, "How long, O Lord? Will You forget me forever? How long will You hide Your face from me?" (Psalm 13:1). But even then, when all seems lost, our confidence must remain in the goodness and faithfulness of God who is still at work and who will eventually deliver us from our affliction. Knowing this, the psalmist followed up his plaintiff lament and said, "But I have trusted in Your lovingkindness; My heart shall rejoice in Your salvation. I will sing to the Lord, Because He has dealt bountifully with me" (vv. 5-6).

9

What God May Be Up to in Our Suffering

In his book, *When There Are No Easy Answers*, John S. Feinberg (Professor of Biblical and Systematic Theology at Trinity Evangelical Divinity School) shares the profound impact tragedy can have on one's faith. He describes the agony he and his dear wife felt when she was diagnosed with an incurable, genetically transmitted disease. The transparent descriptions of his personal suffering and how he went through a phase where he even questioned God's goodness spoke deeply to my heart. He also shared how well-meaning clichés were of no help to his tormented soul; and how simple faith in the promises of God combined with a willingness to rejoice in the simple daily demonstrations of God's goodness brought much-needed comfort. He spoke of how God's all-sufficient grace was never stored up in advance, but was always available just when he needed it most.

But I especially found his *Appendix* on *The Uses of Affliction* to be most helpful. And I share them with you in light of the subject at hand, that you, too, might be encouraged by God's providential workings in your life. He asks, "How, then, might God use affliction positively in the life of the righteous sufferer? There are many ways, and I have divided them into ten basic categories."[11] Here is his list (minus the expanded explanations and biblical documentations):

- Affliction provides an opportunity for God to manifest His power.
- God may use affliction to remove false boasting.
- God allows afflictions at least in part to show Satan genuine faith.
- God uses affliction as an opportunity to demonstrate to believers and nonbelievers the concept of the body of Christ.
- In a number of ways affliction in the life of the righteous can and does promote holiness.
- Sometimes God uses suffering to prepare us for future ministry and blessing.
- God also uses pain and distress to prepare us for further trials.

- God uses suffering in the lives of the righteous to prepare them for judgment of their works.
- God may use our afflictions as a basis for ultimately exalting us.
- God may use afflictions as a means to take us to be with Himself.[12]

We can see some of the aforementioned uses of affliction in the heart-wrenching story of the Spafford family of Chicago, Illinois. Horatio Spafford arranged an extended family vacation to Europe to see the Old World—something his wife in particular longed to do. After traveling by train to New York in preparation for their trip across the Atlantic, Horatio received notice that he needed to return to Chicago to handle an unexpected business problem. Rather than canceling the trip, he decided to send his wife and two daughters on ahead. As they embarked on the *SS Ville du Havre*, he assured them he would be along shortly. With his party reduced by one, he was able to upgrade his family's cabin accommodations in the bow of the ship—a change that later proved disastrous.

On November 22, 1873, the *SS Ville du Havre* was struck by a western-bound British ship, the *Loch Earn*, cutting the bow of the *Ville du Havre* almost in half. Within twelve minutes, the ship sank, carrying 226 passengers to a watery grave in the Atlantic. Hearing of the accident, Horatio prayed that his family had survived. But seven days after the tragedy at sea, Mrs. Spafford (and fifty-six other survivors) landed at Cardiff, Wales. There she sent a telegram to her husband that simply said: "Saved alone." Their four daughters all drowned: Annie (11), Maggie (9), Bessie (6), and Tanetta (2).

As you might imagine, the shock and the subsequent grief was almost unbearable for both Horatio and his wife Annie, who were both genuine believers who dearly loved and served Christ. Spafford wired his wife and asked her to wait there in England and he would catch the next ship. One biographer described what happened next:[13]

> As the voyage began, Spafford braved the cold winter wind and walked to a spot near the vessel's bow, staring out across the water. He kept watch at the position for most of the trip. It was while standing at the ship's rail that the words of his friend, Dwight Moody, came back to the grieving man. One of the evangelist's most famous quotes might well have done more than lift Spafford's spirits at the moment: it might just have inspired him to compose a poem that became his most public legacy of faith.

Moody had once told thousands at revival meetings, "Someday you will read in the papers that D.L. Moody of East Northfield is dead. Don't you believe a word of it! At that moment I shall be more alive than I am now; I shall have gone up higher, that is all, out of this old clay tenement into a house that is immortal—a body that death cannot touch, that sin cannot taint; a body fashioned like unto His glorious body."

As Spafford considered the reality of death and the surety of his faith, he began to realize that his daughters were very much alive. He would not see them again for a while, but they were now better off than any of those on the ship around him. As this thought welled up in his soul, the captain of the ship called out to him, "Mr. Spafford, we are nearing the spot where your daughters now rest."

The downcast father suddenly felt the girls' spirits around him. Rather than cry, he smiled. He was flooded with a sense of peace. For the first time in more than a week, he felt the Lord's hand on his shoulder. Rushing to his cabin, Spafford picked up pen and paper and quickly jotted down the words that were suddenly in his heart:

> When peace, like a river, attendeth my way,
> When sorrows like sea-billows roll;
> Whatever my lot, Thou hast taught me to say,
> It is well, it is well with my soul.

Horatio Spafford's hymn, *It Is Well With My Soul*, has become the testimony of countless thousands who have experienced the soul-satisfying peace of God's presence in the darkest hours of tragedy. The full lyrics of the hymn are as follows:

> *When peace, like a river, attendeth my way,*
> *When sorrows like sea billows roll;*
> *Whatever my lot, Thou hast taught me to say,*
> *It is well, it is well with my soul.*

> *Refrain*
> *It is well with my soul,*
> *It is well, it is well with my soul.*

> *Though Satan should buffet, though trials should come,*
> *Let this blest assurance control,*
> *That Christ hath regarded my helpless estate,*
> *And hath shed His own blood for my soul.*

> *My sin—oh, the bliss of this glorious thought!—*
> *My sin, not in part but the whole,*
> *Is nailed to the cross, and I bear it no more,*
> *Praise the Lord, praise the Lord, O my soul!*

> *For me, be it Christ, be it Christ hence to live:*
> *If Jordan above me shall roll,*
> *No pang shall be mine, for in death as in life*
> *Thou wilt whisper Thy peace to my soul.*

But, Lord, 'tis for Thee, for Thy coming we wait,
the sky, not the grave, is our goal;
Oh, trump of the angel! Oh, voice of the Lord!
Blessed hope, blessed rest of my soul!

And Lord, haste the day when the faith shall be sight,
The clouds be rolled back as a scroll;
The trump shall resound, and the Lord shall descend,
Even so, it is well with my soul.

To be sure, when the storms of life are the greatest, our strength must come from the living Lord Himself who rests comfortably with us in our little boat that is seemingly ready to sink. It was with this in mind that I wrote the following poem (derived from an exposition of Matthew 14:22-33):

Life is filled with gale force winds that cause the waves to roar;
And like the men of Galilee we strain against the oar.

With billows high we cry aloud, "Oh Lord, where have You gone?"
Then He whispers through the squall, "I've been here all along."

Oh we of little faith, why doubt? Why give our hearts to fear?

For when the tempest trials blow, 'tis then we must draw near!

For in the wind of every storm a Sovereign eye doth see,
The waning faith and broken hearts of those like you and me.

And with His outstretched hand of love, He reaches down to save,
All who trust in Him alone; for us His life He gave!

So when the tumults o'er us roll, let's thank Him for the gale,
For in His love He caused the storm, 'twas He who set the sail.

10

Final Words of Encouragement

Though "the sufferings of Christ are ours in abundance" (2 Cor. 1:5), we can find relief knowing that Satan's rule is only temporary and our glorious King will one day return in power and great glory to put at an end once and for all to evil and suffering. The tragedies and atrocities of life should animate our hatred of Satan and sin, and never our anger toward God. The inevitable sorrows of life in this sin-cursed world are opportunities for us to long all the more for glory when "He will wipe away every tear from [our] eyes; and there will no longer be *any* death; there will no longer be *any* mourning, or crying, or pain; the first things have passed away" (Rev. 21:4). But until that glorious day, we can find comfort knowing that God has not abandoned us in our sufferings, for indeed in His permissive providence He has ordained to allow them to accomplish

His eternal purpose to bring glory to Himself and eternal life to those He has saved by His grace.

Through life's storms we must trust our glorious God for who He is, for His goodness and justice remain untarnished in all that He does. Moses said, "The Rock! His work is perfect, for all His ways are just; a God of faithfulness and without injustice, righteous and upright is He" (Deut. 32:4). He is the thrice-holy God praised by the seraphim (Isa. 6:3)—holiness being the all-encompassing attribute of God that portrays His hidden glory, His infinite otherness, His incomprehensible transcendence, His consummate perfection, and His moral purity. For this reason the apostle John says, "God is Light, and in Him there is no darkness at all" (1 John 1:5). And it is only in Him that we can find light in the darkness of evil.

For this reason Peter comforted the persecuted saints when he said, "Humble yourselves under the mighty hand of God, that He may exalt you at the proper time, casting all your anxiety on Him, because He cares for you" (1 Peter 5:7-6). Even in the hopelessness and helplessness of excruciating sorrow and gratuitous evil, we can rest assured in God's promise that He will never leave us nor forsake us (Heb. 13:5). Moreover, when we look closely, in every trial we can see His tender mercies and goodness put on display, often in ways that are unexpected—a glimpse of the glory to come. And then, in the midst of the pain, we will find comfort and experience the soul-satisfying joy of His presence, consistent with His promise that He will never give us more than we can bear (1 Cor. 10:13), His grace will always be sufficient (2 Cor. 12:9), and His throne is always accessible, "Therefore let us draw near with confidence to the throne of grace, so that we may receive mercy and find grace to help in time of need" (Heb. 4:16).

Truly, "The Lord's lovingkindnesses indeed never cease, for His compassions never fail. *They* are new every morning; Great is Your faithfulness" (Lam. 3:22-23). In light of these great truths we can affirm the inspired words of James when he says: "Consider it all joy, my brethren, when you encounter various trials, knowing that the testing of your faith produces endurance. And let endurance have *its* perfect result, so that you may be perfect and complete, lacking in nothing" (James 1:2-4).

Armed with these great truths, and comforted by them, our heart can echo the apostle's great doxology of faith and say:

> Oh, the depth of the riches both of the wisdom and knowledge of God! How unsearchable are His

judgments and unfathomable His ways!
For who has known the mind of the Lord, or who became His counselor?
Or who has first given to Him that it might be paid back to him again?
For from Him and through Him and to Him are all things.
To Him *be* the glory forever. Amen" (Rom 11:33).

Endnotes

1 David F. Wells, *Above All Earthly Pow'rs: Christ in a Postmodern World* (William B. Eerdmans Publishing Company, Grand Rapids, Michigan / Cambridge, U.K., 2005), 3-4.

2 *The MacArthur Study Bible* (Thomas Nelson, Nashville, TN, 1997), 694.

3 Robert Duncan Culver, *Systematic Theology; Biblical and Historical* (Christian Focus Publications, Ltd., Geanies House, Fearn, Ross-shire, Great Britain, 2005), 302.

4 John S. Fineberg's book, *The Many Faces of Evil: Theological Systems and the Problems of Evil, Revised and Expanded Edition* (Crossway, Wheaton, Illinois, 2004) is helpful in this regard.

5 D. A. Carson, *How Long, O Lord? Reflections on Suffering and Evil*, Second Edition (Baker Academic, Grand Rapids, Michigan, 2006), 219.

6 Robert Duncan Culver, *Systematic Theology; Biblical and Historical* (Christian Focus Publications, Ltd., Geanies House, Fearn, Ross-shire, Great Britain, 2005), 302.

7 (John Calvin, *Institutes of the Christian Religion* (Peabody, MA; Hendrickson Publishers, Inc., 2008), 137.

8 Ibid., 138.

9 Thomas Watson, *All Things For Good* (The Banner of Truth Trust, Carlisle, Pennsylvania, First published 1663, Reprinted 2001), 55-56.

10 Ibid., 60-61.

11 John S. Feinberg, *When There Are No Easy Answers: Thinking Differently About God, Suffering, and Evil* (Kregel Publications, Grand Rapids, MI, 2016), 137.

12 Ibid., 138-149.

13 Ace Collins, *Stories Behind the Hymns that Inspire America* (Zondervan, Grand Rapids, Michigan, 2003), 110-111.

www.ingramcontent.com/pod-product-compliance
Lightning Source LLC
Chambersburg PA
CBHW050605300426
44112CB00013B/2075